Financial Freedom Demystified: What the Rich Know About Money That Others Don't

Michael D. Lind

All rights reserved. No part of this publication may be reproduced, distributed or transmitted in any form or by any means, including photocopying, recording or other electronic or mechanical methods, without the prior written permission of the publisher, except in the case of brief quotations embodied in critical reviews and certain other noncommercial uses permitted by copyright law.

Copyright © (Michael D. Lind) (2024)

PART I	9
PART II	31
PART III	43
PART IV	65
PART V	86
CONCLUSION	103

INTRODUCTION
The journey to financial freedom

Envision if you may wake up each morning knowing that your budgetary concerns are history. Envision yourself getting a charge out of a glass of coffee on a sun-filled overhang as you gradually organize your day, having realized the long-aspired objective of money related freedom. This remains a far-off dream for numerous. But for a modest bunch, it's their day-to-day presence. What information do they have that the others need? Which insider facts do the well off keep so safely that it appears like they play a diverse game?

The key to figuring out such perplexes is this book, "Financial Freedom Demystified: what the rich know about money that others don't". It's an investigation of the contemplations and behaviors that make the well off distinctive from the rest of the populace.

At the begin of our story, Emily, a single mother of two, is working unimaginably difficult at her calling but is having monetary troubles. Indeed in spite of the fact that she worked exceptionally difficult, having a steady salary felt unattainable. Emily stands in for the millions of individuals who have to appear for their labors since they are stuck in the cycle of winning and buying. A way better approach has to exist, she realized.

While scrutinizing her neighborhood bookshop one critical evening, Emily came over a brochure for a money related class. It claimed to unveil privileged insights more often than not as it was known by the affluent and effective advertising experiences into the rich era and organization. In spite of her skepticism, she made the choice to go. Her life was irreversibly influenced by that choice.

She met coaches at the occasion who advertised individual accounts of how money related proficiency and clever contributing have changed their lives. She found that the key to monetary flexibility is to make your cash work for you or maybe than attempting to make more cash. She came to get it the centrality of monetary proficiency, the control of compound intrigued, and the viability of budgeting. Most altogether, she found that anybody who was arranged to think about and put the concepts into use may receive an affluent attitude.

Emily seen a change in her life as she put these strategies into use. She begun sparing, paid off obligation, and inevitably made judicious ventures. Her travel from budgetary hardship to steadiness serves as a motivational illustration of the esteem of monetary literacy.

Similar to how Emily's class served as her direct, this book serves as yours. It's expecting to clarify the precepts that the affluent take after and illustrate how you can utilize them in your claim life. You'll find the procedures for making different income streams, the esteem of contributing, and the craftsmanship of budgeting. You will learn the mental change

ations required to overcome monetary impediments and enter a plenteous environment.

However, this isn't basically another dry-theory budgetary handbook. It's a street outline outlined to help you in coming to your monetary destinations, total with doable activities and down to earth cases. This book has something for everybody, whether your objectives are to decrease obligation, spare investment funds for a critical buy, or create a solid contributing portfolio.

Are you arranged to take charge of your future monetary circumstance? Are you prepared to learn the privileged insights the affluent keep and consolidate them into your possessive life? This is where the way to monetary autonomy starts. Together, let's rearrange cash so you can accomplish your monetary goals.

Accompany me on this life-changing experience. It's time to realize your wealth potential and achieve the monetary autonomy you so well merit. Your future self will be grateful.

PART I

FOUNDATION OF WEALTH

1. WHY FINANCIAL EDUCATION MATTERS

Financial education is essential for both individual and societal prosperity in a society where economic activity is king. Financial literacy is still one of the most underappreciated topics in formal education systems worldwide, despite its great significance. Fostering a financially secure and stable society requires an understanding of the importance of financial education.

I. The Basis of Knowledge in Finance

Those who receive financial education are better able to handle their personal finances because they have the information and abilities needed. This entails being aware of fundamental financial ideas including debt management, investing, saving, and budgeting. A person's financial well-being is improved when they are able to make well-informed decisions regarding their spending, investments, and future savings.

II. Financial Knowledge for Personal Empowerment

One effective strategy for empowering oneself is financial education. It gives people the power to steer their own financial course and lessens reliance on outside counsel that might not always be optimal. For example, learning how to create a budget will help you avoid going over your spending limit and accumulate money for unexpected expenses. Understanding retirement planning and investments enables people to take control of their financial destiny and avoid relying exclusively on unpredictable sources like social security or pensions.

III. Reducing Financial Stress and Debt

In the consumer-driven society of today, debt is a prevalent problem. Although credit cards, loans, and mortgages are essential components of contemporary financial life, they can cause serious financial hardship if used improperly. People who are financially educated are better able to comprehend the long-term effects of debt on credit scores as well as its interest rates and payback periods. People can steer clear of the traps of excessive borrowing and the stress that goes along with it by learning how to manage their debt well.

IV. Encouraging Growth and Stability in the Economy

Financial education also plays a significant role in the economic development and stability of communities and countries. Financially literate people make wiser financial decisions, which can result in higher investment levels, higher savings rates, and more frugal spending habits. Because there is more money available for company investments, innovation, and development, this in turn promotes economic growth.

V. Diminishing Inequality and Poverty

Poverty and inequality may be decreased through financial education. Financial literacy resources are typically inaccessible to low-income individuals and families, hence exacerbating the poverty cycle.

By giving them financial education, we may enable them to save for the future, participate in chances that will enhance their financial situation, and handle their money more wisely. As a result, resources and money may be distributed more fairly, fostering societal stability.

VI. Strengthening the Safety of Customers

A populace with greater financial literacy is better able to make educated decisions, avoid scams and predatory behavior, and navigate the complicated financial landscape. Customers may choose the best solutions for their needs and prevent being duped by pushy marketing strategies by being aware of the terms and conditions of financial goods like loans and insurance.

VII. Technology's Place in Financial Education

The financial education landscape has changed as a result of the rise of digital technology. Obtaining financial information is now simpler than ever thanks to smartphone apps, online courses, and tools for financial management. With the help of these technologies, people may receive individualized instruction, study at their own speed, and immediately apply the knowledge to their daily life. Apps for budgeting, for example, can assist users in tracking their savings and expenditures in real time, offering prompt feedback and promoting improved financial practices.

VIII. Financial Literacy in the Classroom

Building a financially literate society requires incorporating financial education into school curricula. We educate children and young adults for the financial obligations they will face as adults by teaching them the fundamentals of money management. Early financial education demystifies complicated subjects like credit and investing and encourages the development of sound financial habits like budgeting and saving. Schools have a significant impact on young people's financial destiny by providing them with the tools they need to succeed in the job market.

IX. Lifelong Learning and Financial Education

Financial education isn't a one- time event but a lifelong process. The financial geography is constantly evolving, with new products, technologies, and profitable conditions arising regularly.

Nonstop literacy is essential to stay informed and acclimatize to these changes.

Workshops, forums, online courses, and tone- study can help individuals keep their financial knowledge up- to- date and applicable. In conclusion, financial education is a vital element of particular and societal well- being.

It empowers individualities, reduces financial stress, promotes profitable stability, and fosters social equivalency.

As the financial world grows increasingly complex, the need for robust financial education becomes more pressing.

By prioritizing financial knowledge in our educational systems and particular lives, we can make a more financially secure and prosperous future for all. Whether you are a pupil just starting out, a professional dogging to enhance your financial wit, or a retiree planning for your golden times, financial education is an inestimable asset. It's no way too early or too late to start learning. Invest in your financial education moment, and reap the benefits for a continuance.

2 . MINDSET AND MONEY

The Power of Mindset

Unleashing a Healthier Relationship with money

Our mindset plays a profound part in shaping our relationship with wealth. It influences how we earn, save, spend, and invest.

A healthy mindset can lead to financial stability and freedom, while a defective use can affect stress, debt, and recession. In this composition, we'll explore the intricate connection between wealth and mindset, and give practical strategies for cultivating a healthier relationship with wealth.

The failure Mindset

A failure mindset views wealth as limited, fostering fear and anxiety. This leads to overspending, hoarding, or avoidance. People with a failure mindset frequently believe that
 - wealth is hard to come by
 - There is no way enough
 - They'll have no way to achieve financial stability.

This mindset creates a tone- fulfilling vaticination, leading to financial struggles and stress.

The Money Mindset

On the other hand, a money mindset sees wealth as a tool for growth and openings,

promoting confidence and wise financial opinions. People with an wealth mindset believe that
- wealth is a means to an end, not the end itself
- There is always enough
-financial stability is attainable.

Cultivating A Money Mindset

To cultivate a wealthy mindset, fete and challenge negative beliefs and allowed patterns. Replace them with empowering declarations, fastening on gratefulness, positivity, and tone-worth. Exercise awareness, contemplation, or journaling to increase mindfulness of your studies and feelings.

Develop a Growth Mindset

Develop a growth mindset, embracing financial education and tone- enhancement. Set clear pretensions, prioritize requirements over wants, and practice aware spending. Focus on progress, not perfection.

Let Go of Emotional Spending

Let go of emotional spending, using wealth to fill voids or seek confirmation. rather, use wealth to enhance gests , connections, and particular growth. Exercise tone- compassion and tone- mindfulness to fete emotional triggers.

Cultivate tolerance, Discipline, and Resilience

Cultivate tolerance, discipline, and adaptability, feeling that financial progress is a marathon, not a sprint. Celebrate small triumphs, learning from lapses and staying married to your vision.

Practical Strategies

1. Exercise gratefulness Reflect on the effects you are thankful for each day.
2. Reframe negative studies Challenge limiting beliefs and replace them with empowering declarations.
3. Set clear pretensions Prioritize requirements over wants and produce a financial plan.
4. Exercise aware spending: Be present and purposeful with your financial opinions. 5.

Cultivate tone- mindfulness Fete emotional triggers and allowed patterns. By transubstantiation your mindset, you will unleash a further purposeful and fulfilling relationship with wealth.

You will make purposeful financial opinions, aligning with your values and bournes . Embrace the power of mindset, and you will be on your way to a brighter financial future.

Remember, financial freedom is a trip, not a destination.

3. UNDERSTANDING ASSETS AND LIABILITIES

Understanding assets and liabilities is pivotal for achieving financial freedom. Financial freedom refers to having enough means to induce income that exceeds one's charges, allowing an individual to live comfortably without counting on traditional employment.

To achieve this, one must develop a clear understanding of what means and arrears are, how they impact one's financial health, and strategies for managing them effectively.

Defining assets and liabilities means are coffers that have profitable value and can give unborn benefits. They can induce income, appreciate in value, or give mileage. means can be palpable, like real estate, vehicles, and outfit, or impalpable, like stocks, bonds, patents, and intellectual property.

Cash and cash coequals, similar as savings accounts and instruments of deposit, are also considered means because they can be fluently converted into cash. arrears, on the other hand, are financial scores that an individual or business owes to others.

They represent claims on an existent's means and must be settled over time through the transfer of wealth, goods, or services. Common exemplifications of arrears include mortgages, auto loans, credit card debt, pupil loans, and any other kind of particular or business debt.

The part of assets and liabilities in financial health

To understand how means and arrears impact financial health, it's helpful to look at the balance distance, a financial statement that provides a shot of an existent or association's financial position at a given time.

The balance distance equation is

Assets = Liabilities Equity or net worth, is the difference between means and arrears.

Positive equity means that the value of means exceeds arrears, indicating a healthy financial situation.

Negative equity, where arrears surpass means, signals financial torture and implicit solvency issues. structure Wealth through means

For achieving financial freedom, accumulating means is essential. Then are some strategies for erecting wealth through means

1. Investing In stocks, bonds, collective finances, and real estate can induce returns that make wealth over time. Diversification, which

involves spreading investments across different asset classes, can help manage threats.

2. Real Estate retaining property can give rental income and implicit appreciation in value. Real estate is frequently considered a stable, long-term investment.

3. Savings Building an emergency fund in a high-yield savings regard can give financial security and liquidity. Regular savings also enable investment in other means.

4. Business Power retaining a business can induce significant income and equity. Successful businesses can appreciate in value and give a steady slice of profit.

5. Intellectual Property Creating intellectual property, similar as patents, trademarks, or imprints, can induce unresistant income through royalties or licensing freights.
Managing arrears

Effectively managing arrears is inversely important for financial freedom. Then are strategies to keep arrears in check

1. Debt Reduction Paying down high-interest debt, like credit card balances, should be a precedence. Reducing debt lowers interest payments and frees up cash for saving and investing.

2. Strategic Borrowing Not all debt is bad. Strategic borrowing, similar to taking out a mortgage to buy a home or a loan to start a business, can be salutary if the espoused finances are used to acquire means that appreciate in value or induce income.

3. Refinancing Refinancing high-interest debt to lower interest rates can reduce the cost of borrowing and accelerate debt prepayment.

4. Budgeting Creating and clinging to a budget helps control charges and ensures that arrears are manageable relative to income.

5. Emergency Fund Maintaining an emergency fund can help the need to take on high- interest debt in case of unanticipated charges.

Achieving Financial Freedom

To achieve financial freedom, it's essential to produce a positive gap between means and arrears. This involves

1. Adding means Continuously investing in income- generating and appreciating means. This builds wealth over time and creates multiple aqueducts of income.

2. dwindling arrears Reducing debt and avoiding gratuitous borrowing. This minimizes financial scores and interest payments.

3. Monitoring Progress Regularly reviewing your financial situation to insure that means are growing and arrears are under control. conforming strategies as demanded grounded on financial pretensions and request conditions.

4. Financial Education Continuously learning about particular finance, investing, and wealth operations to make informed opinions.

Understanding means and arrears, and effectively managing them, is the foundation of financial freedom. By fastening on erecting means and minimizing arrears, individualities can produce a strong financial foundation that supports a life of independence and security.

PART II

BUILDING WEALTH

4. INCOME STREAMS

Achieving financial freedom requires a strategic approach to generating income. counting on a single income source can limit your financial growth and increase vulnerability to profitable downturns. Diversifying your income aqueducts can give stability, security, and openings for wealth creation.

Then are crucial income aqueducts to consider

1. Primary Income This is your main source of income, generally from a payment or stipend.
2. Passive Income earns wealth without laboriously working, through investments, rental parcels, or tip- paying stocks.
3. Side Hustles Supplement your primary income with part- time gambles, freelancing, or entrepreneurship.

4. Investments Generate returns through stocks, bonds, real estate investment trusts(REITs), or peer- to- peer lending.

5. Reimbursement Income Earns wealth by renting out parcels, outfit, or means.

6. Royalty Income Receive payments for intellectual property, creative workshop, or inventions.

7. tip Income Earn regular payments from shares in tip- paying companies.

8. Online Income Monetize digital chops, produce and vend online products, or induce announcement profit.

9. Retirement Income Plan for sustainable income sources in withdrawal, similar as pensions, appropriations, or withdrawal accounts.

Diversifying your income aqueducts offers multitudinous benefits

- Reduces financial threat
- Increases earning implicit
- Enhances financial security
- Provides openings for wealth creation
- Supports long- term financial pretensions

To achieve financial freedom, aim to produce multiple income aqueducts, allocating
- 30% to primary income
- 20% to unresistant income
- 20% to side hustles
- 15% to investments
- 15% to other income streams

Flash back, erecting different income aqueducts takes time and trouble.

Start by
- Assessing your financial situation
- Setting clear pretensions
- Exploring new income openings
- Investing in particular development
- Monitoring and conforming your strategy.

By cultivating a diversified income sluice portfolio, you will be better equipped to achieve financial freedom, rainfall profitable storms, and produce a prosperous financial future.

5. INVESTMENT BASICS

Achieving financial freedom requires a well-planned investment strategy. Investing wisely can help grow your wealth, achieve long- term financial pretensions, and secure your financial future.

These are the investment basics to get you started:
1. Set Clear Goals Define your financial objects, threat forbearance, and time horizon.
2. Understand Asset Classes Familiarize yourself with stocks, bonds, real estate, goods, and cash.
3. Diversification Spread investments across asset classes to minimize threat.
4. Risk Management Balance threat and implicit returns grounded on your pretensions and threat forbearance.
5. Long- Term Focus repel short- term request oscillations and stay married to your strategy.
6. Bone- Cost Comprising Invest regularly to reduce timing pitfalls.
7. Low- Cost Investing Minimize freights and charges.

8. duty-Effective Investing Consider duty counter accusations and optimize your strategy.

9. Regular Portfolio Rebalancing Maintain your target asset allocation.

10. Education and Research Continuously learn and stay informed.

Investment Vehicles

1. Stocks Represent power in companies.

2. Bonds Represent debt scores with regular income.

3. Index finances Track a specific request indicator.

4. Exchange- Traded finances(ETFs) Tradeable finances tracking an indicator. 5. collective finances Professionally managed investment portfolios.

6. Real Estate Invest in property or real estate investment trusts(REITs).

7. Retirement Accounts use duty- advantaged accounts like 401(k), IRA, or Roth IRA.

Investment Strategies

1. Value Investing Focus on underrated means.

2. Growth Investing Target high- growth eventuality.

3. tip Investing Emphasize regular income.

4. Index Investing Track request performance.

5. Bone- Cost Comprising Invest regularly.

By learning these investment basics and strategies, you will be well on your way to achieving financial freedom.

- Stay disciplined and patient
- Continuously educate yourself
- Avoid emotional opinions
- Examine and acclimate your strategy.

Investing wisely can help you make wealth, achieve financial independence, and secure your financial future. Start your investment trip moment!

6. BUDGETING AND SAVING

 Attaining financial freedom requires a strategic approach to budgeting and saving. Effective budgeting enables you to manage your finances, prioritize spending, and allocate coffers towards your pretensions. Saving, on the other hand, builds wealth, provides security, and energy investments.

Then is a comprehensive companion to budgeting and saving for financial freedom

Budgeting

1. Track Charges Cover income and charges to understand spending habits.
2. classify Spending Allocate charges into requirements(casing, food), wants(entertainment), and debt prepayment.
3. Set Financial pretensions Prioritize short- term and long- term objects.
4. Assign probabilities Allocate income into orders(50 requirements, 30 wants, 20 savings).
5. Acclimate and upgrade Regularly review and optimize your budget.

Saving

1. Emergency Fund Save 3- 6 months' charges for unanticipated events.
2. Short- Term Savings Allocate for specific pretensions(recesses, down payments).

3. Long- Term Savings Focus on withdrawal, wealth accumulation, and big- ticket particulars.
4. High- Yield Savings use high- interest accounts for optimal growth.
5. Avoid life Affectation Direct redundant finances towards savings and investments.

Strategies

1. Pay Yourself First Prioritize savings and investments.
2. Automate Savings Set up automatic transfers.
3. Cut Charges Identify areas for reduction.
4. Increase Income Pursue fresh sources or raises.
5. Avoid Debt Minimize high- interest debt and produce a debt prepayment plan.

Stylish Practices

1. Regularly Review Assess budget and savings progress.
2. Avoid Impulse Purchases Exercise delayed delectation.
3. influence Technology use budgeting apps and tools.
4. Educate Yourself Continuously learn about particular finance.

5. Stay Disciplined Maintain long- term focus and commitment.

By learning budgeting and saving, you will be well on your way to achieving financial freedom. Flash back to stay flexible, patient, and informed, and you will unleash a brighter financial future.

PART III

MANAGING MONEY WISELY

7. MANAGING DEBT

Getting out of debt is one of the most important things you can do to become financially free. Debt could be a big problem when you're trying to save money and build up your wealth. This is a complete guide to getting out of debt and being financially independent:

Figuring Out Debt

1. Types of Debt: Tell the difference between bad debt (like credit cards and personal loans) and good debt (like homes and school loans).
2. Debt Snowball: Put your bills in order by balance or interest rate on them.
3. Debt Avalanche: Start with loans with high interest rates.

Tips for Dealing with Debt

1. Make a budget. Write down all the money you earn and spend so you know how much you can put toward paying off your debt.
2. Get a pay raise or find new ways to make money to pay off your debts faster.
3. Reduce Expenses: To increase cash flow, find areas that can be cut.
4. Debt Consolidation: Merge bills into one credit card or loan with a reduced interest rate.
5. Engage in Creditor Negotiation: Ask for reduced payments or interest rates.

6. Pay More Than the Minimum: Steer clear of deferring paying off debt.
7. Reduce Credit Card Costs: Steer clear of new credit card debt.
8. Think About Balance Transfers: Transfer high-interest debt to a credit card with a lowered interest rate.
9. Get Professional Assistance: Speak with a debt management group or credit counselor.

Top Techniques

1. Keep an eye on credit reports: Verify correctness and follow changes.
2. Avoid New Debt: During repayment, avoid from taking on new loans.
3. Establish an Emergency Fund: Put money away for unforeseen costs.
4. Remain Disciplined: Keep your long-term devotion and attention.
5. Educate Yourself: Keep up your understanding of debt management and personal finance.

How to Become Financially Independent

1. Debt Freedom: Honor major debt payback accomplishments.
2. Wealth Building: Set away money for savings and investments.
3. Financial Security: Take pleasure in less worry and peace of mind.
4. Greater Flexibility: Take advantage of opportunities and make choices free from debt restrictions.
5. Long-Term Success: Make sure your finances are safe.

You can achieve financial freedom by becoming an expert in managing your debt and upholding discipline. Maintaining your composure, knowledge, and commitment can help you to open a more promising financial future.

8. SMART TAX STRATEGIES

Developing wise tax strategies is important to reaching financial independence. By maximizing savings and lowering liabilities, comprehending and putting these principles into practice can have a major impact on one's financial health.

In order to help people and groups understand the complexity of the tax code and get closer to financial freedom, we'll look at some important tax tactics here.

1. Retirement Accounts with Tax Advantages

Tax-advantaged retirement plans, such as 401(k)s, IRAs, and Roth IRAs, are among the best methods to lower your tax burden and prepare for the future.

- 401(k) Plans: Pre-tax contributions to conventional 401(k) plans lower your yearly taxable income. As a result, you pay less in income taxes, both state and federal. Furthermore, a lot of companies match employee contributions, which basically gives you free money for retirement.

- Individual Retirement Accounts, or IRAs: Conventional IRAs work similarly to 401(k)s in that they let you make pre-tax contributions and postpone paying taxes on your investment gains until you're retired. Conversely, withdrawals from a Roth IRA after retirement are tax-free even when the account is filled with after-tax money. This can be especially helpful if you expect to eventually fall into a higher tax bracket.

2. HSAs, or health savings accounts

HSAs provide three tax benefits: tax-deductible contributions, tax-free growth, and tax-free withdrawals for approved medical bills. Those with high-deductible health plans (HDHPs) can start these accounts. HSAs are an effective tool for long-term wealth building and healthcare savings because unused money carries over from year to year.

3. Tax-Advantageous Investments
You may be able to keep a larger part of your investment gains by making tax-efficient investments.

- Index funds and exchange-traded funds (ETFs): These investment vehicles usually produce smaller taxable events because they distribute capital gains less frequently than actively managed funds.

- Tax-Loss Harvesting: This tactic lowers your total tax bill by selling lost investments to balance the gains from winning ones.

- Municipal Bonds: Interest earned on municipal bonds is often exempt from state and local taxes as well as federal income tax. High earners may find this especially beneficial.

4. Making Use of Tax Credits

Compared to deductions, which simply lower your taxable income, tax credits directly lower the amount of tax you owe and may be more helpful. The following are some important tax credits to be aware of:

- Earned Income Tax Credit (EITC): This tax credit, which is available to working families and people with low to moderate incomes, can lead to a sizable refund.

- Child Tax benefit: Families with dependent children may be able to receive major relief from this benefit.

- Education Credits: The Lifetime Learning Credit and the American Opportunity Credit can be used to partly defray the expense of a college education.

5. Self-Employed Individuals' Deductions

Many deductions are available to self-employed people, which can greatly lower their taxable income.

- Home Office Deduction: You might be eligible to write off costs linked with the portion of your house that is used solely for business.

- Health Insurance Premiums: Self-employed people are qualified to write off the expense of their families' and their own health insurance premiums.

- Retirement Contributions: Compared to standard IRAs, self-employed people can give more to SEP IRAs or Solo 401(k)s.

6. Donations to Charities

Contributions to eligible nonprofits can meet one's desire for philanthropy while also offering tax benefits. In order to optimize the tax benefits:

- Donate Appreciated Assets: Think about giving away valuable stocks or other assets instead of cash. You can avoid paying capital gains tax by subtracting the asset's fair market value.

- Donor-Advised Funds: With these funds, you can contribute to charity, get a tax benefit right away, and then gradually disperse the money to different charities.

7. Trust Administration

A well-crafted estate plan might lessen your heirs' tax burden.

- Gift Tax Exclusion: You are exempt from gift taxes on gifts to recipients up to a particular annual amount. This may be a calculated move to lower the amount of your taxable estate.

- Trusts: Setting up trusts helps reduce estate taxes while managing and safeguarding your assets. For instance, assets held in irrevocable trusts may be excluded from your taxable estate.

8. Tax Diversification

To allow yourself flexibility in retirement, tax diversification entails distributing your savings among many account types (taxable, tax-deferred, and tax-free).

By letting you select the retirement account that would allow you to take out the largest tax savings, this technique can help you reduce your overall tax liability.

9. Maintaining Precise Records

To maximize deductions and credits, thorough and precise record-keeping is essential. This entails preserving bank statements, receipts, and other records of every transaction that could have an impact on your tax status. Maintaining accurate records enables you to support your claims and steer clear of problems during an audit.

10. Expert Counseling

The laws pertaining to taxes are intricate and dynamic. Working with a tax expert can guarantee that you're maximizing the tax savings options and offer individualized assistance. They can also guide you through more difficult circumstances like beginning a business, managing an inheritance, or juggling several sources of income.

Effective tax planning is crucial for anyone hoping to become financially independent. You may decrease your taxes and keep more of your income by using tax-advantaged accounts, investing wisely, taking advantage of credits and deductions, and making future plans.
 To further improve your tax plan and assist you in navigating the intricacies of the tax system, maintain precise records and seek professional advice.

In addition to lowering present tax obligations, comprehending and putting these solutions into practice lays the groundwork for long-term stability and financial well-being.
A comprehensive strategy that combines astute tax planning with general financial planning is necessary to achieve financial freedom. By being diligent and making wise decisions, you can

improve your tax position and get closer to your financial objectives.

9. PROTECTING YOUR WEALTH

Many people want to be financially independent, but safeguarding your wealth is just as crucial to this process.

Having enough cash on hand, investments, and savings to support your desired family and personal lifestyle is the definition of financial freedom.

It also entails expanding those resources while effectively managing them. These are a few tactics to safeguard your assets and guarantee your financial stability in the long run.

1. Make Investment Diverse

Sound investing fundamentals include diversification. Risks can be reduced by distributing your investments over a variety of asset classes, including stocks, bonds, real estate, and commodities. In the event that a market section underperforms, gains could be offset by underperforming ones. In addition to safeguarding your wealth, diversification increases growth potential and moves you closer to financial independence.

2. Emergency Savings

Having an emergency fund is essential to safeguarding your assets. Unexpected costs can quickly drain your money, such as unexpected medical bills, auto repairs, or job loss. Having an emergency fund, which usually equates to three to six months' worth of living expenses, acts as a safety net to prevent you from taking premature withdrawals from retirement accounts or investments, which can result in penalties and cause havoc with long-term goals.

3. Protection From Insurers

A further important component of wealth protection is having enough insurance. Insurance for property, health, life, and disability protects against large-scale financial losses.

Life insurance provides for your family in the event of your death, disability insurance substitutes income in the event that you are unable to work, and property insurance safeguards your valuables from theft or damage. Health insurance pays for medical bills.

Having the right insurance protects your goals of financial freedom from unanticipated events.

4. Trust Administration

To safeguard your riches and make sure your final desires are carried out, estate planning is crucial. A complete estate plan consists of a power of attorney, trusts, wills, and healthcare directives. These contracts specify who will handle your affairs, how your assets should be divided, and your healthcare choices in the event that you become incapacitated. By reducing taxes and legal complications, estate planning helps you save more of your fortune for your beneficiaries.

5. Financial Scheduling

Protecting money requires careful tax preparation. Your financial well-being can be greatly impacted by knowing and using tax regulations.

By lowering your tax burden and maximizing tax deductions and credits, tax-loss harvesting, and other strategies, you can increase the amount of money in your investment and decrease your tax liability. You can be sure you're taking full advantage of these opportunities and adhering to tax laws by speaking with a tax professional.

6. Consistent Financial Evaluation

The key to preserving and safeguarding wealth is to examine and modify your financial strategy on a regular basis. Financial objectives, individual circumstances, and market conditions all fluctuate over time.

Periodically reviewing your investments helps make sure that your risk tolerance, savings rate, and investment plan match your long-term goals and current circumstances. By being proactive, you may make well-informed modifications that help you stay on track for financial freedom.

7. Steer clear of heavy debt

Debt loads that are too high can endanger financial independence. Your savings and investment returns may be negatively impacted by interest payments on loans and credit cards. Make paying off high-interest debt your top priority, and refrain from taking on additional debt. Reducing borrowing expenses and offering financial flexibility when required can also be achieved by using credit responsibly and keeping a high credit score.

8. Education about Finances

The secret to safeguarding and increasing your wealth is ongoing education in finance. Making wise financial decisions is facilitated by learning new investment techniques, getting up to date on market developments, and comprehending the fundamentals of personal finance. Develop your financial literacy and resilience by learning from books, classes, and expert guidance.

To sum up, safeguarding your wealth is a complex process that includes emergency savings, insurance, diversification, tax preparation, estate planning, ongoing education, and regular financial evaluations. You may reduce risks, protect your investments, and move closer to financial independence by putting these methods into practice.

PART IV

ADVANCED CONCEPTS

10. ENTREPRENEURSHIP

Numerous people hail entrepreneurship as an important means of reaching financial independence.

In contrast to traditional work, which generally offers a fixed pay and little room for advancement, entrepreneurship enables people to use their imagination, provocation, and inventiveness to produce companies that have the eventuality to make large sums of wealth.

Then are some tips for achieving financial freedom through entrepreneurship as well as the styles for making this business successful.

The Mindset of an Entrepreneur

The correct mindset is essential for achieving financial freedom through entrepreneurship. A threat- taker, an inventor, and a problem- solver are entrepreneurs.
When others see obstacles, they see openings, and they're set to put in the time, wealth, and

trouble necessary to make their dreams come true. This way of thinking is pivotal for prostrating the unknowns and difficulties that arise when launching and expanding a business.

Chancing Possibilities

The first step in being a successful entrepreneur is to find a promising company. This could be an opening in the request, a slice-edge good or service, or a creative system to enhance presently available options.

To comprehend consumer requirements, request demand, and competitiveness, in-depth request exploration is essential.

A strong business plan that describes the business model, target request, marketing tactics, and financial protrusions is erected upon the exploration that has been done. Creating a Robust Base A solid base is essential for any business bid. This entails forming your company's legal structure, similar as a pot, LLC, cooperation, or sole procurement.

The ramifications for responsibility, taxation, and functional freedom vary depending on the structure. Getting enough wealth is also pivotal, whether it comes from loans, investors, crowdsourcing, or particular savings. Having the right finance guarantees you have the means needed to launch and grow your company.

Creating a Business Strategy

A thorough business plan serves as a road chart for your entrepreneurial trials. It should include a description of your company's objects, plans, and necessary conduct.

A precisely considered business plan gives your company a clear path and aids in carrying capital. It consists of financial estimates, product or service immolations, organizational structure, marketing strategies, and request analysis.

Maintaining your focus and inflexibility in the face of shifting conditions is assured by routinely assessing and streamlining your company plan.

Putting together an important team

A single entrepreneur can not come financially independent. Developing a solid platoon is pivotal to growing your company.

Your business's performance can be greatly impacted by hiring talented and impulsive people who match your capacities and partake in your vision. In order to be an effective leader, one must assign tasks, promote a healthy work terrain, and offer chances for professional development.

Innovation, productivity, and expansion can be fostered by a motivated and cohesive pool.

Expanding the Enterprise

Getting your business to the coming position is essential to reaching financial independence.
This entails developing your consumer base, growing your operations, and boosting deals.

Diversifying your product or service immolations, breaking into new requests, establishing strategic alliances, and exercising technology to boost productivity are all exemplifications of scaling strategies.

Careful growth operation is necessary to maintain quality and satisfy guests. Handling wealth One of the most important corridors of entrepreneurship is financial operation.

Maintaining accurate records of your earnings, expenses, and gains is pivotal for making well-informed business choices.

Account software can expedite this procedure and offer perceptive data on the financial well-being of your company. Having enough cash on hand to pay for operating charges and make investments in expansion prospects is guaranteed by effective cash inflow operation.

Likewise, reinvesting and reserving a portion of your earnings for extremities contribute to the long- term health of your association. Promotion and Identity Attr acting and keeping guests depends on strong branding and marketing.

Creating an important brand identity that appeals to your target followership helps set your company piecemeal from rivals. Your visibility and reach can be expanded by exercising a variety of marketing platforms, including social media, dispatch marketing, content marketing, and SEO.

Feting the conditions and preferences of your guests and furnishing value on a regular basis fosters reprise business and brand fidelity. Accepting Innovation The secret to successful entrepreneurship is invention. Keeping up with current specialized developments and assiduity trends enables you to constantly introduce and acclimatize.

This could be enforcing innovative business strategies, expanding your line of goods or services, or using technology to ameliorate customer relations. Accepting inventions keeps you competitive and enables you to satisfy changing customer demands.

Mentoring and networking Creating a network of peers, instructors, and business connections can be a great way to get advice and ideas. Online groups, professional associations, and assistance events can all present networking openings.

In particular, instructors can give advice grounded on their gests, aiding you in prostrating obstacles and coming to wise conclusions. Your entrepreneurial trip can be accelerated and new chances can arise by girding oneself with a helpful network.

Tenacity and fiber

Being an entrepreneur has numerous obstacles. Adaptability and continuity are essential rates for prostrating obstacles and being devoted to your objects. You may stay motivated in trying times by keeping a positive mindset, learning from miscalculations, and conforming to new situations.

Long- term success and good are also told by maintaining a work- life balance and admitting little accomplishments.

A lively and conceivably fruitful route to financial independence is handed by entrepreneurship. Entrepreneurs can establish prosperous and financially independent businesses by embracing an entrepreneurial mindset, seeing openings, laying a solid foundation, creating detailed business plans, and no way stopping conniving.

Indeed though the path demands commitment, perseverance, and hard work, entrepreneurship is a charming option for anyone looking to achieve financial independence because of the implicit prices.

11. REAL ESTATE INVESTING

Investing in real estate has long been allowed to be one of the stylish paths to financial independence. Real estate, in discrepancy to numerous other investment options, provides a range of advantages, including influence eventuality, duty benefits, capital appreciation, and steady income inflow.

An in- depth examination of how real estate investing can lead to financial freedom is handed then.

The Advantages of Investing in Real Estate

1. Generation of Passive Income

The possibility of unresistant income is one of the most charming features of real estate investing. Whether they're marketable or domestic, rental parcels bring in wealth each month. In addition to paying for conservation, property operation freights, and mortgage payments, this harmonious cash inflow constantly leaves a fat that can be reinvested or employed to pay for particular musts. This unresistant income can come a substantial source of financial independence over time as rental income rises in line with request rates.

2. Gratitude

The value of real estate generally increases over time. Although there may be short-term differences due to request oscillations, real estate values have generally shown an upward long-term tendency. Your net worth rises as a result of this appreciation's construction of equity. Enhancing appreciation rates and making smart investments in high-growth regions can also quicken the process of getting financially independent.

3. Tax Advantages

There are several duty benefits for real estate investors. Operating costs, real estate levies, and mortgage interest are subtracted from rental income. deprecation is a non-cash deduction that lowers taxable income by allowing you to write down the property's value over time. likewise, real estate investors can reinvest gains without facing immediate duty responsibility by using procedures like the 1031 exchange to defer capital earnings levies. Because of these duty advantages, real estate is a duty-effective investment that increases overall gains.

4. Use influence openings in real estate are distinct.

You can have lesser control over a larger asset base than you could with only your cash if you use espoused wealth to finance the purchase of real estate.

For illustration, you can buy a property for five times your original investment with a 20 down payment.

This influence increases possible pitfalls as well as benefits, but it can greatly increase your capability to accumulate wealth if used wisely.

Real Estate Investing

1. Acquire and Maintain Buying parcels and holding them for a long time to benefit from appreciation and reimbursement profit is known as the steal- and- hold approach. This long- term strategy can produce steady, regular cash inflow and is comparatively unresistant. opting parcels in sought- after areas with high rental demand and appreciation eventuality is pivotal.

2. Acclimate and Turn Purchasing homes that are underrated, fixing them up, and also reselling them for a profit is known as fix and flip. This approach necessitates a thorough grasp

of the original request as well as a sharp eye for property value and additional costs. Fix and flip real estate investing can yield significant short-term returns, but it also carries an advanced threat, necessitates active operation, and demands real estate and construction knowledge.

3. REITs, or real estate investment trusts Investing in Real Estate Investment Trusts(REITs) provides exposure to real estate without taking direct property power for individuals who would rather take a more laissez- faire approach. Companies that enjoy, manage, or finance income- producing real estate across a range of diligence are known as REITs. They're a liquid and fluently accessible choice for real estate investing because they're intimately traded and pay tips.

4. Temporary lodging Compared to conventional long- term settlements, short- term settlements like those announced on Airbnb or VRBO have the eventuality to yield further rental income. This tactic works especially well

in sightseer locales and populated places where there's a strong need for short- term lodging. It does, still, necessitate aggressive operation, marketing enterprise, and adherence to indigenous laws.

5. Real Estate for Commercial Use Compared to domestic real estate, investing in marketable means, similar as office structures, retail stores, and artificial parcels, can yield larger returns and longer parcel terms. Marketable real estate can offer diversification and a harmonious income sluice, but it generally requires lesser investments and further intricate administration. Managing threat and plying Care Conditions for successful real estate investing include threat operation and expansive scrutiny.

Important effects to suppose about are - request exploration To make wise investment opinions, one must have a thorough understanding of the original frugality, property valuations, rental rates, and request circumstances. -financial Analysis

To make sure you make wise investments that support your financial objectives, precisely examine possible returns, cash inflow estimates, and backing possibilities.

- Property operation icing tenant pleasure, conserving property value, and optimizing rental income all depend on competent property operation. Either you or a professional property operation company can handle this.

-Diversification You can reduce the pitfalls connected with request and profitable downturn changes by spreading your real estate effects across a variety of property kinds and locales.

Creating Wealth and Reaching Financial Independence An accessible and profitable route to financial independence is handled by real estate investing. Real estate investors have the eventuality to accumulate significant wealth over time by employing strategic investment ways, using duty advantages, producing unresistant income, and benefiting from property appreciation. Prudent operation, thorough planning, and thorough disquisition are essential for success.

The unresistant income and erected- up equity in your real estate portfolio can give you the stability and financial independence you need to reach your financial freedom objectives as it expands. To add up, real estate investing is an effective strategy for generating wealth and achieving financial independence. Through appreciation of the advantages, application of effective tactics, and threat operation, investors can construct a sturdy and varied real estate portfolio that yields steady returns and enduring financial stability.

PART V

SUSTAINING FINANCIAL FREEDOM

12. LONG-TERM FINANCIAL PLANNING

A typical ambition is to become financially independent, however for many people, this goal is unattainable since they haven't made long-term financial plans. Having enough income to pay your bills without actively working for it and being free from financial constraints to make decisions about your life is what it means to be financially free.

A strategic approach to wealth management, investing, and long-term wealth growth is necessary to achieve this goal. The key elements of long-term financial planning will be discussed in this article, along with how they help people achieve financial freedom.

1. Identify Your Financial Objectives

Clearly defining your financial goals is the first stage in any long-term financial plan. Since the term "financial freedom" is vague, it's critical to define it specifically for you. It could mean retiring early for some, building up a specific amount of cash, or leading a stress-free lifestyle for others.

Establish SMART goals—specific, measurable, achievable, relevant, and time-bound. This clarity will direct your preparation and sustain your motivation.

2. Evaluate Your Present Financial Condition

You must have a comprehensive awareness of your existing financial condition before you can create a plan. This entails assessing your income, expenses, liabilities, and assets. Create a thorough budget and net worth statement to see where your money is going. This evaluation shows you where you need to improve and helps you understand where you are right now.

3. Establish and Adhere to a Budget

One essential tool for managing finances is a budget. It aids in the effective distribution of your income, enabling you to save and invest while maintaining your standard of living. Divide your spending into needs (such housing and utilities) and wants (like eating out or entertainment) to start. To make sure you are consistently saving money and not overspending, keep track of your expenditures and make adjustments as needed.

4. Establish an Emergency Reserve

An emergency fund serves as a safety net for finances, helping to pay for unforeseen costs like auto repairs, medical emergencies, and job loss. This reserve ought to be sufficient to cover three to six months' worth of living expenditures. When unplanned needs come up, having an emergency fund keeps your long-term financial plan on track by keeping you from taking out loans or investing money.

5. Get Rid of Debt

The accumulation of debt, particularly credit card debt with high interest rates, can pose a serious obstacle to reaching financial independence. Create a debt repayment plan that prioritizes paying off high-interest debt first and only makes the bare minimum payments on other obligations. To progressively pay down your debt, think about employing strategies like the snowball or avalanche tactics. You can use such payments for savings and investments after your debt is under control.

6. Make Sensible Investments

A crucial element of long-term financial planning is investing. It enables your money to increase over time, beating inflation and assisting in the accumulation of wealth. To spread risk and increase possible returns, diversify your assets among a range of asset classes, including stocks, bonds, and real estate.

7. Make a Retirement Plan

Saving for retirement is essential to having financial freedom. Establish a savings plan to help you reach the amount of money you'll need in retirement to maintain the lifestyle you choose. Make use of retirement funds and, if offered, employer-matched contributions. Make sure your retirement plan stays on track with your goals and life changes by reviewing and adjusting it on a regular basis.

8. Guard Your Resources

A crucial component of long-term financial planning is insurance. It assists in shielding your assets against unforeseen circumstances that can jeopardize your financial objectives. Health, life, disability, and property insurance are among the insurance types to take into account. Having sufficient coverage guarantees that you can stick to your financial plan and won't be bankrupted by unanticipated events.

9. Make Tax Plans

You should have a strategy in place for handling taxes because they can have a big impact on your financial plan. Recognize how your income and investments will be taxed, and make use of tax-deferred or tax-exempt investment accounts. To make the most of your tax status and steer clear of any shocks that can jeopardize your financial security, speak with a tax specialist.

10. Track and Modify Your Strategy

Financial planning is a continuous process rather than a one-time occurrence. Make sure your financial plan is in line with your objectives on a regular basis. Modify it if something in your personal life, the market, or your financial status changes. Establish regular check-ins, such once a year or twice a year, to evaluate progress and make any required modifications.

11. Consult a Professional

Although managing oneself is possible, seeking advice from a financial advisor can offer more knowledge and direction. Financial advisers can aid with complex financial problems, provide individualized advice, and assist with investing ideas. Their expertise and experience can support you in overcoming obstacles and improving your financial planning efforts.

12. Develop Financial Self-Control

Finally, developing a disciplined financial approach is essential for sustained success. Respect your savings and investing goals, stick to your budget, and refrain from making rash purchases. Maintaining your focus on your objectives and making steady progress toward financial freedom are made possible by practicing financial discipline.

To achieve financial freedom, long-term financial planning is necessary. You can put yourself on the path to financial independence by setting clear objectives, evaluating your current circumstances, making a budget, setting up an emergency fund, paying off debt, investing sensibly, making retirement plans, safeguarding your assets, paying taxes, keeping an eye on your plan, getting expert assistance, and developing discipline. Financial freedom is achievable with a well-structured strategy, but it takes time, dedication, and constant work.

13. TEACHING FINANCIAL LITERACY TO THE NEXT GENERATION

Teaching financial literacy to the next generation is crucial for equipping young individuals with the knowledge and skills needed to achieve financial freedom. Financial literacy encompasses understanding how money works, including how to earn, manage, invest, and save it effectively. By instilling these principles early, we empower young people to make informed decisions that can lead to long-term financial stability and independence.

1. Understanding Basic Financial Concepts

The foundation of financial literacy begins with understanding basic concepts such as budgeting, saving, investing, and debt management. Young people should learn how to create and maintain a budget, distinguishing between needs and wants, and the importance of living within their means. A budget helps track income and expenses, preventing overspending and fostering a habit of saving.

Saving is another fundamental concept. Emphasizing the value of setting aside a portion of income for future needs, emergencies, and goals encourages a culture of financial discipline. Introducing concepts like the time value of money, where saving early can lead to significant growth through interest and compound returns, can motivate students to prioritize saving.

2. Introducing Investment Strategies

Investing is a key component of achieving financial freedom, and understanding its principles can set the stage for future success. Teaching young people about different investment vehicles, such as stocks, bonds, and mutual funds, helps them grasp the potential for growing their wealth.

Emphasize the importance of diversification to spread risk and the impact of long-term investing. Utilizing simulations or virtual trading platforms can provide hands-on experience without real financial risk.

Educating students about the principles of risk and return, as well as the concept of passive income through dividends or interest, prepares them for making informed investment decisions. Encouraging them to think about their long-term financial goals and how investments can play a role in reaching them fosters a proactive mindset.

3. Debt Management and Credit

Understanding debt and credit is essential for financial stability. Teach young people about the differences between good debt (such as a mortgage or student loans) and bad debt (such as high-interest credit card debt). Explain the impact of interest rates and the importance of paying off debt on time to avoid accumulating unnecessary interest and damage to credit scores.

Credit scores play a crucial role in financial health, affecting the ability to secure loans and favorable interest rates. Educate students on how credit scores are calculated, the importance of maintaining good credit, and strategies for building a positive credit history. This knowledge helps them make responsible borrowing decisions and understand the long-term implications of their financial behavior.

4. Real-World Applications

To reinforce financial literacy, incorporate real-world applications into learning.
Encourage students to manage a small budget, track their spending, or even start a small investment portfolio. Real-life scenarios, such as planning for a large purchase or dealing with unexpected expenses, can help students apply theoretical knowledge to practical situations.

Providing opportunities for experiential learning, such as internships in financial institutions or workshops with financial experts, offers valuable insights into how financial principles are applied in various careers. Additionally, involving parents and guardians in the educational process ensures that financial literacy is reinforced at home.

5. Encouraging a Growth Mindset

Promoting a growth mindset about financial learning is vital. Financial literacy should be viewed as an ongoing journey rather than a one-time lesson.

Encourage curiosity, continuous learning, and adaptation to changing financial landscapes. This mindset fosters resilience and adaptability, essential traits for navigating financial challenges and achieving long-term financial freedom.

In summary, teaching financial literacy to the next generation involves equipping young individuals with the knowledge and skills to manage money wisely, make informed investment decisions, and handle debt responsibly. By incorporating these principles into education and daily practices, we prepare young people to achieve financial freedom and build a secure financial future.

CONCLUSION

ACHIEVING AND MAINTAINING FINANCIAL FREEDOM

Achieving and maintaining financial freedom isn't just about accumulating wealth—it's a mindset and a lifestyle. At its core, financial freedom means having control over your money rather than letting it control you. The journey begins with setting clear, attainable goals and crafting a strategic plan that aligns with your values and ambitions. Building a solid foundation involves budgeting wisely, saving consistently, and investing intelligently. Embracing these principles not only helps you create a safety net but also positions you to seize opportunities that come your way.

However, the path to financial freedom doesn't end with reaching a particular milestone. It requires ongoing discipline and adaptability. Regularly reviewing and adjusting your financial strategies ensures that you stay on course despite life's inevitable twists and turns. Embrace a growth mindset, and remain open to learning and evolving with changing financial landscapes. This adaptability is crucial for navigating economic fluctuations and personal life events.

Moreover, maintaining financial freedom involves balancing short-term desires with long-term goals. Prioritizing needs over wants, avoiding excessive debt, and making informed decisions will help preserve your wealth and reinforce your financial stability. It's also about nurturing a healthy relationship with money—one that values security and purpose over mere accumulation.

Ultimately, achieving and sustaining financial freedom empowers you to live life on your own terms. It offers the liberty to pursue passions, spend time with loved ones, and contribute meaningfully to causes you care about.

Remember, financial freedom is not a final destination but a continuous journey of mindful management and intentional living.

By staying proactive and focused, you can not only achieve but also maintain a state of financial well-being that enriches every aspect of your life.